Start an Automated Online Business

Start an Automated Online Business: Turning Your Passions Into Millions

John A. Estrella

Start an Automated Online Business:
Turning Your Passions Into Millions

Paperback: 978-1-990135-00-2
Kindle: 978-1-990135-01-9
Audible: 978-1-990135-02-6

Editing by Suzanne Baal
Cover design by Luisito Pangilinan

Agilitek Corporation
Markham, Ontario, Canada

agilitek.com

About the Author

John A. Estrella, PhD, CMC, PMP, coaches solopreneurs how to start, scale, and sell profitable automated online businesses using proven strategies and systems. He consistently strives to realize more and higher achievements. With a proven track record of working with creativity, integrity, and drive, he earns respect, inspires cooperation, and exceeds expectations.

Dr. Estrella founded consulting and online companies. He currently serves as the Academic Coordinator of the Project Management Certificate at The Chang School of Continuing Education at Ryerson University. He contributes to the community as Scouts Canada's International Commissioner. He was recognized with the Queen Elizabeth II Diamond Jubilee Medal for his volunteer work with Canada's youth.

His educational background includes a BSc (Dean's List) and an MSc (Teaching Fellow & Scholar; 4.0 GPA) degrees in Computer Science. The Project Management Institute (PMI) Educational Foundation awarded him a scholarship for his PhD in Organization and Management (4.0 GPA). Continuing education includes Conversational French (Toronto) and Nonprofit Board (Harvard).

Connect with Dr. Estrella at https://johnestrella.com.

Automated Online Business Books

Start an Automated Online Business: Turning Your Passions Into Millions

Paperback: 978-1-990135-00-2
Kindle: 978-1-990135-01-9
Audible: 978-1-990135-02-6

Scale an Automated Online Business: Unlocking and Perfecting Profitability

Paperback: 978-1-990135-03-3
Kindle: 978-1-990135-04-0
Audible: 978-1-990135-05-7

Sell an Automated Online Business: Maximizing the Selling Price

Paperback: 978-1-990135-06-4
Kindle: 978-1-990135-07-1
Audible: 978-1-990135-08-8

Solopreneur Programs

Apply to our programs by visiting our website.
https://agilitek.com/solopreneur

Dedication

To my wife, Maria, and my children, Joshua, Jacob, and Clara, this book is dedicated to all of you.

—John A. Estrella

Table of Contents

Preface

After clicking on so many online ads for free checklists, presentations, and webinars, I got so frustrated for wasting so much of my time.

First, several of them present shallow and regurgitated materials. There is no breadth and depth. They experienced some success applying a technique that they learned somewhere from someone, and they expect that you will be able to replicate their success. With a rented Lamborghini in the background, they attempt to project an image of success. Second, they only focus on one aspect of the problem, not the end-to-end process of running a thriving business. Third, their companies do not necessarily contribute to significant and long-lasting value for their clients. They are selling bandages, knowing that their customers need surgery.

My view of a business is different. While some entrepreneurs like to build a business that will become a public company someday, I want to start companies that will become profitable within a few months. Other entrepreneurs find thrills in hustling with investors to fund their ventures. In contrast, I like to bootstrap a company so that I can retain majority control. Several solopreneurs spend long hours running their business and creating social media content to remain in the spotlight. For me, I let my automated online business run on its own so that I can enjoy life with my family, pursue what I want, and contribute my fair share to the community.

I've decided to write a book trilogy about starting, scaling, and selling an automated online business with a desire to share with those who will listen. You cannot build a sustainable business by merely knowing how to run an incredible Facebook ad campaign. Creating content for YouTube or recording podcasts continuously to get more likes, shares, and comments will not do the trick. You need to master the entire process, and more importantly, you need to integrate them seamlessly together.

This book focuses on the first portion of the trilogy by teaching you how to start an automated online business so that you can turn your passions into millions. We begin by examining your passions and how you can use them to solve a problem for someone. In return, they will compensate you fairly for your service. This process requires a thorough understanding of your target customer so that you can position your product, and therefore your business, for success.

We build a solid foundation by formalizing the business, creating a scalable pipeline to serve the customers, and optimizing the entire customer experience. When you reach this point, you would have built an automated online business that can thrive without you while remaining profitable. It will be reasonably profitable so that you can continue to let it run or sell it to another entrepreneur. This venture is a solo operation, an automated online business for a solopreneur.

Thank you for joining me on this journey. I'll be your mentor. I will show you the way and steer you away from common mistakes, but you have to do the work. Reach out to me anytime at https://johnestrella.com, and I'll do my best to help you. We are on this journey together.

Even if you are intellectually smart, don't let your mindset fail you. That's the biggest challenge, which I know you can overcome. I'm counting on you. Good luck!

Acknowledgment

Dan Poynter inspired me to write my first book. Over the years, I picked up valuable entrepreneurial insights from Timothy Ferriss, Chris Guillebeau, and John Warrillow. When it comes to business strategy, I subscribed to the expertise of Alan Weiss, Mike Michalowicz, Michael E. Gerber, Richard S. Ruback, and Royce Yudkoff. I'm so thankful for their wisdom.

Behind the scenes, a mountain biker opened the door for me to achieve a business breakthrough. Never in a hundred years would I have imagined that a former bartender will show me how to put the business pieces together and that a former US Navy SEAL holds the key to sell with confidence, care, and integrity. Joined by a world-class team of mindset experts and paid advertising gurus, I was able to crack the million-dollar puzzle. They shall remain nameless for now but rest assured I owe them my sincerest gratitude.

START-AOB #

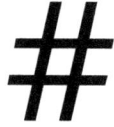

INTRODUCTION

Everyone has something they love doing. It's possible
to bootstrap an automated online business that can
generate a million dollars or more each year in any
industry, doing what you love. If you want to make six
figures, or even just enough to replace your current
salary, that's fine too. All you need is a reliable Internet
connection, and you can manage your business
independently, a solopreneur, from anywhere in the
world. We are not talking about a fly-by-night
operation. This venture is a legitimate and sustainable
business that brings you joy and respect while
providing significant value to your customers. This
well-engineered business can generate predictable
profits for years, or you can sell it at a premium to a
private buyer or a well-established corporation.

Although several opportunities exist for starting an online business, and some of them can be very lucrative, most are transitory, parasitic, inconsequential, or not scalable. Examples include social media influencers, Amazon sellers, affiliate marketers, and online coaches, to name just a few. While they are Internet businesses, they are not automated and require considerable effort and attention from their owners.

Social media influencers need to continually feed the machine by writing blogs, posting stories, creating videos, and recording podcasts. It's a full-time job, and Instagram or YouTube can shut down the accounts anytime. Amazon sellers invest substantial capital upfront in placing bulk orders to offshore suppliers. If that's not already a deterrent, Amazon owns the customer lists, not the seller, and the online stores can be closed anytime.

Affiliate marketers and drop-shippers require a sizable audience to sell another company's products. Customer acquisition costs often far surpass the sales commissions. Lastly, others follow the traditional trade-time-for-money scheme even though they do the work remotely on their laptops. They call themselves digital nomads. Although it's slightly better than a regular 9-5 office job, it's not scalable and requires ongoing effort.

But there is a way to make a good living doing what you love without the risk of the other options' immense time commitment. If you follow the principles and concepts outlined in this book, you will be in a much better position. What you need are the principles and ideas we call the *Millionaire Manifesto*.

Get paid well for doing something you are passionate about by solving one and only one major problem for someone else. The solution must be very profitable, easily repeatable, and highly valuable. Focus on customers who are ready, willing, and able: prepared for a solution to their problem, keen to find a solution, and able to pay for it.

Throughout this book, we will only refer to the solution as the "product" even though it can be a product, service, or result. The product must take the customer to the end, not merely provide them with a piece of the puzzle or walk them through a step in the process. Based on preliminary market research, create a unique selling proposition (USP) and build a minimum viable product (MVP). Engineer a simple but highly optimized sales and marketing pipeline while continually improving the product based on customer feedback.

Impossible? Not really. Let's get started!

★ ★ ★ ★ ★

Please take a selfie or video with this book and share it on social media and Amazon. Feel free to tag me and keep me updated on your progress.

#solopreneur #aob-book #aob-trilogy

Thanks, John Estrella

CHAPTER 1

MESH YOUR PASSION WITH REMUNERATION

Reflect on the following questions to start your journey of creating an automated online business. Respond based on how you genuinely think and feel, and not based on someone else's expectations of you or how you want to be perceived by others. If answered truthfully, these questions will help frame your product and uncover potential issues that could prevent you from achieving your business goals.

- What do you enjoy doing?
- How much do you want to make?
- What are your self-limiting beliefs?
- Can you master your mindset?

By meshing your passion with your remuneration, you will greet each day with energy and enthusiasm as you pursue your mission in life. As a bonus, your customers will compensate you generously for your efforts. There is nothing more fulfilling than doing what you enjoy and co-creating your customer's happiness. Along the way, you are making a difference in the lives of others while building a respectable, sustainable, and lucrative business.

Let's explore these questions in more detail.

What do you enjoy doing?

Some people know what they enjoy exactly and can keep just doing it without noticing the time. They are in the flow, and they are truly blessed to have found their happiness. Other people find it more elusive. They don't know what they want precisely. Somewhere in between, some appreciate multiple things, to varying degrees, some more than others. If this is you, you need to focus on one thing that you genuinely enjoy. It should be something that you like doing, more than any other activity.

Don't think about money for a moment. Ignore whether you have formal credentials or professional experiences. For now, focus on identifying that one thing that you genuinely enjoy. What's your happiest moment from when you were a child? What's your most memorable positive experience from school? Was there a project at work that made you feel immensely proud and happy? Is there a hobby that you can imagine yourself doing for the rest of your life, or can't wait to get back to each weekend?

When you are browsing websites, what topics do you typically read? What videos do you watch online? Who are you following on social media, and what do you like about them? What bothers you that you think others also experience, and you'd like to find a solution for it? Was there a traumatic experience that you or a family member went through, and you want to help others avoid or cope with it?

After identifying your passion, the next step is to think about fair compensation for your efforts.

How much do you want to make?

Don't worry about your exact product for now. You also have to resist the temptation to filter by thinking that a certain amount is too small or too big. We'll get into that later. For example, maybe you say that you enjoy plants, and you want to make about $60,000 per year. Or, you want to spend more time on your favorite activity, scuba diving, and you want to make $100,000 per year.

Considering that the median household income in the U.S. is $63,688, it's unfathomable for most people even to consider making $1,000,000 per year. However, 18.6 million people in the US are millionaires, the highest globally, proving that it is entirely possible. Sure, it might have taken them years to accumulate that wealth, but the first step is to break it down to get a sense of how their journey would look if earned in just one year.

If you divide $1,000,000 by 12 months or 52 weeks, that's $83,333 per month or $19,231 per week. You'd need to make about $2,740 every single day for the entire year. For someone used to working 40 hours per week, expecting to make $481 per hour may be unrealistic. Sure, some surgeons or lawyers may charge that much as their hourly rate, but that would still mean working 40 billable hours every week, all 52 weeks in a year, without any time off for vacation, illness, professional development, and other obligations. It's not a viable business model for most people. Therefore, the second step is not to trade your time for money.

Although professional athletes make millions, an average person can't become a fantastic basketball or baseball player overnight. Even if you give most people time, they don't have the will or talent even to attempt it. It's better to think like an actor or a singer. Unlike professional athletes who rely on their abilities to perform and earn, consider the concept of creating a product once and then selling it multiple times, like a movie or a song. Multiply yourself by packaging your product or service so that it can be built once and sold over and over again—no more trading time for money! There is a systematic approach to do this, and we'll dive deeper into it later.

For now, decide how much you want to make each year. There is no right or wrong choice. It's unique for everybody. Imagine a scenario where your life is perfect. You live in your dream home, you drive your favorite car, and you get to do whatever you want, whenever you want. How much do you need to make per month to have that lifestyle? The only caveat is the third trick, which is to be reasonably realistic.

Everything takes time and effort. If you are making $60,000 per year now, it's possible to replace that income with an automated online business. The learning curve for the first $5,000 will be very steep. However, once you get there, you can easily double or triple it.

From personal experience, my first venture took just under four years from zero (just an idea, $100,000+ in investment, no corporation) to my first sale. In the fifth year, the venture reached a key milestone, $100,000+ in annual revenue. The business venture crossed the $83,333 monthly revenue threshold by year six, signifying a million-dollar business benchmark. A second venture took only a year to build by learning from that experience, starting with sweat equity and less than $10,000 invested for start-up costs. That venture earned an average of $5,000 per month in revenue shortly after launch and surpassed $100,000 in annual revenue within a year. This business venture is entirely possible!

Unless you have done it before, it will take longer to figure it out, and you will likely waste money on costly mistakes. With the valuable insights outlined in this book, or better yet with guidance from a mentor or coach, you'll be able to realize the results faster with fewer issues. There are endless mechanical methods to increase your revenue, such as upsell, cross-sell, optimizations, paid ads, and affiliates, to name a few. But to go from $0 to $1,000,000 requires much more than mechanical methods. You need to rally your mental strength as well, which is what we'll talk about next.

What are your self-limiting beliefs?

After successfully coaching several first-time Amazon bestselling authors, it quickly became evident that self-limiting beliefs made a profound difference between those who could publish their books from scratch after four weeks and those who couldn't even finish a chapter. Irrational and unhealthy beliefs can prevent you from realizing your full potential. These beliefs will not only significantly impact your personal life, but they will also drastically impede your professional growth. Self-limiting beliefs can morph into self-fulfilling prophecies if left unchecked.

Start reflecting on your personal beliefs. While these beliefs come in many forms, they revolve around compensation, age, credential, experience, and fear. People who have not made a six-figure income may think they do not deserve $100,000 per year. Do you think starting entrepreneurship in your forties puts you at a disadvantage? Not really.

Vera Wang began designing clothes professionally at 39, Ray Croc stumbled into the MacDonald brothers at 51, and Colonel Sanders started KFC in this forties. Even a lack of degree and experience did not deter billionaires from pursuing their passions: Richard Branson, Michael Dell, and

Larry Ellison. Regardless of their circumstances, they overcame their fears of starting their business. They pushed through even though they don't know what to do if they get stuck.

Then, identify your beliefs about others. My family will think I'm crazy. Here we go again, another business venture that will fail. No one will buy my product. Naysayers will say that I'm a fraud. By the way, impostor syndrome is a legitimate psychological pattern, so seek professional help if it's holding you back.

Lastly, examine your beliefs about the world. The Internet is already too saturated for another online business. It's better to make money in real estate compared to digital products. Be aware of these beliefs, and remember that they are not facts!

Write down all of your self-limiting beliefs. Similar to how you identified your passion, be honest with yourself. What self-limiting beliefs do you have about yourself? About others? About the world? Challenge each one of your assumptions and assertions. If you dig deeper, you'll realize that those self-limiting beliefs are just inside your head.

The good news is you have control over them. You need to give yourself permission to challenge and eradicate these self-limiting beliefs! Ask the questions, "So, what?" and "What if I'm wrong?" after each self-limiting belief. As easy as it may sound, it often requires a simple change of perspective to go past your self-limiting beliefs.

Now that we have discussed self-limiting beliefs, the next step is to consider a related topic, mastering your mindset.

Can you master your mindset?

If you look around the internet or social media, you'll find many tips and tricks on nurturing a positive mindset. However, being a decisive entrepreneur trumps them all. Keep taking the next step by avoiding analysis paralysis.

By not making a decision quickly, you'll end up consuming energy to rationalize why you shouldn't do something instead of moving forward to get to the next milestone. If you cannot or will not decide, you'll remain stuck, and there will be no progress. In contrast, if you choose, even if it is wrong, you can always find ways to correct it later. You'll most likely find ways to solve it directly or skirt around it to get to the next step. Regardless, it's far superior to going nowhere.

If an author aims for a perfect book, it will never get published. If a programmer desires ideal software, it will never get released. Likewise, if an entrepreneur insists on perfecting a product before selling it, there will be no revenue and no opportunity to receive valuable feedback from actual customers. That's why books have a second edition, and software has significant updates. Keep making decisions, and keep moving forward.

You will likely fall at least partly into the analysis paralysis trap. Faced with options, often without enough information, you'll find yourself stuck. You'll use it as an excuse not to move forward. Instead, apply a decisive mindset to focus on what you can do, not on what you cannot control. You may also see yourself making small enhancements and tweaks, hoping to get something perfect. These actions are just an excuse, a delaying tactic because you didn't want to commit to a decision to finish a particular activity. Aim for completion, not perfection.

When you are running paid ads to grow your business, you will likely experience a scarcity mindset, especially if you are spending $10, $25, $100, or $1,000 per day and not making a single sale. That's normal. However, embrace the data and avoid the drama. If you are selling a $100 product, it's perfectly acceptable to let it run for ten days without getting any of that money back. Remember, you only need to sell one product to recover your investment.

It takes time to optimize marketing campaigns, so you need to be patient. It can take Google and Facebook up to a week to fine-tune their algorithms based on your paid ad parameters. To ensure consistency, you probably need to leave it alone for 2-3 weeks to normalize the data. It's great if it works. If not, look at the data, make the necessary adjustments, and start the cycle all over again. It's trial and error, so you need to be organized and decisive about what you will do next. Can you rise above the scarcity mindset? Embrace the data, avoid the drama.

Now that we have covered the essential steps for turning your passion into an income, the next chapter will delve into the technical aspects of creating an automated online business.

★ ★ ★ ★ ★

If you are enjoying this book so far, can you please tell your friends about it via email or social media?

#solopreneur #aob-book #aob-trilogy

Thanks in advance, John

CHAPTER 2

SOLVE A PROBLEM FOR SOMEONE

The first chapter discussed the inward-facing elements of turning your passion into an automated online business. It focused on the owner's passion, desired income, beliefs, and mindset. Also, important considerations are the external-facing components, including defining the ideal customer. However, there are critical foundational components to consider first, which deal with the product itself that the business will sell. Consider these questions:

- What product should you sell?
- How much should the product cost?
- Will it provide enough value to the customer?
- Can the process be repeated efficiently?

Answer these questions in sequence but also understand that this is an iterative process. After you have defined the initial product and settled on an initial price, you may realize that it will not provide enough value to the customer. So, you need to start over, refine the product definition, and adjust the price. Likewise, if the product, price, and value are ideal, but you cannot repeat the process to produce and deliver it efficiently, you will need to iterate again until you achieve a viable product that satisfies all four questions.

Point B

Think about your customers' current situation, Point A, and imagine how their lives will change, their Point B, after purchasing your product. Their transformation from Point A to Point B is the value you will provide to your customers. The bigger the shift, the more they will pay for it. Some transformations are fast and straightforward, while others are complex and slow. Your job as an entrepreneur is to turn complex problems into simple solutions so that your customers can expedite their transformation. It is also imperative to provide them with an end-to-end solution and not just a step in the process.

To help you visualize this process, consider these four scenarios. As a child of music lovers, Gabi started playing guitars at a very young age. Lamar discovered a passion late in life after falling in love with learning languages. Following a more traditional path, Pax built a professional career as a project manager. It didn't take long for Skylar to amass a succulent plant collection after receiving one as a gift from a friend.

To help a friend learn how to play the guitar, Gabi wrote an introductory guitar book and uploaded it to Amazon. It didn't take long before aspiring guitar players started asking for other related instructional books on the classic, electric, blues, jazz, and more. The model is straightforward. Write a book. Upload it to Amazon. Let Amazon handle the entire print-on-demand process to make the book available online, collect the payment, print it on-demand, ship the book, and manage returns, if any. Gabi collects the royalty on the other end.

Although the transformation from Point A to Point B is small, it's a transformation to take someone who cannot play the guitar to play a song on a guitar. As such, the price is low, at $19.99 per book. However, more books mean higher revenue, so there is a clear path to scale the business.

A similar scenario, learning how to speak a new language, can be solved in a slightly different way.

Lamar discovered that schools have been teaching languages the wrong way. The traditional sequence relies on reading, writing, speaking, and listening. It is not uncommon for students to spend years studying a foreign language in high school and college, but they still cannot recognize words and phrases in a normal conversation. Worse yet, native speakers cannot understand these students when they try to say something.

So Lamar developed a new method for learning a language, reversing the learning process. The original method focused on listening and speaking first before learning how to write and read, similar to how babies naturally learn a language. Lamar recorded the elemental sounds of words and showed students how to recognize and produce them. In doing so, they trained their ears to distinguish the sounds' nuances, allowing them to understand what's being said in a conversation more easily. Students can also now produce the same sounds more accurately, which enables others to understand them. Lamar packaged the learning method as an online course that sells for $197 with an upsell of $97.

Unlike Gabi and Lamar, Pax leveraged a professional experience and augmented it with an automated online business. Pax's employer required all project managers to have a particular certification to win government contracts. However, there were no preparation materials available to help project managers prepare for and pass the certification exam. Seeing an opportunity, Pax documented the process, compiled the learning materials, and prepared mock questions. The product sells for $499.99, so just selling one every day translates to about $15,000 in monthly revenue. Because certified project managers can make up to 26% more than non-certified project managers, the transformation from Point A to Point B is more significant. Given that the certification is mandatory, Pax can charge more compared to Gabi and Lamar.

These three examples followed a simple model with varying prices and levels of end-to-end control. Gabi's product is a book that relies on Amazon to market, print, and ship it. If Amazon shuts down Gabi's book, although unlikely, a new process will be required to keep the business running. Market it, get it printed, ship it to a fulfillment center, and let them process the orders.

In contrast, Lamar and Pax offered an electronic product. They can sell the online course multiple times with minimal production cost and without reliance on a third-party platform such as Amazon. Other types of electronic products include templates (presentations, spreadsheets, questionnaires, etc.), software-as-a-service (SaaS) (assessments, calculators, simulators, etc.), and digital libraries (images, sounds, reports, etc.). If you can offer an electronic product, it's the best and most straightforward way to build an automated online business.

However, suppose you don't have the expertise and capital. In that case, you can package someone else's products and services into a viable product to help your customers get to Point B. See how Skylar turned a succulent plant gift into an automated business that keeps on giving. If you were to look at Skylar's Instagram posts and YouTube videos, you would not be able to resist the temptation to start a succulent plant collection. Followers started asking Skylar how to get started, where to buy the succulents, how to take care of them, and what tools to use. As a result, Skylar created free instructional posts and videos. However, each one has a clear call to action: order your starter kit now for $50, shipping included.

Behind the scenes, Skylar arranged with a local wholesaler to fulfill the orders and contacted a manufacturer in China to dropship the tools (small water sprayer and pruning gadgets). When an order arrives, the local wholesaler ships the succulents for $20, and the Chinese manufacturer mails the pruning tools for $10, both directly to the customer. Skylar keeps the remaining $20 as gross profit to pay for web hosting and for a local teenager to post pictures and videos to Instagram and YouTube. In this model, Skylar didn't create the product at all. It's a simple model that sells physical products but with dependencies from suppliers. Regardless, it's another version of an automated online business.

At this point, start thinking about your product and how it will help your customers move from Point A to Point B. The customer's expected transformation allows us to set the initial target price based on the Rule of ⅓, which we will explain shortly. Later, we'll refine the product description, zoom in on the target customer, assess how to enter the market, and figure out where to get the funding to develop the product.

Rule of ⅓

We showed you the Rule of ⅓ in Skylar's succulent plant business model. According to this rule, the business owner should price their product to roughly reserve ⅓ for profit (30-35% of the product's price). Skylar sells each starter kit for $50. $30 goes to suppliers, $3-5 is allocated to maintain the website, and market the product, and Skylar keeps $15-17 for profit from each sale.

Business schools teach various methods to determine how to price products. Here's a simple approach: Figure out how much it will cost to produce the product (labor and materials). If you need to perform part of the work to deliver the product, pay yourself a fair market hourly wage. It can be as low as minimum wage if the task is simple or much higher if it requires specialized skills. Take note that the hourly wage is separate from the ⅓ profit that the owner must carve out first. In doing so, you could replace yourself by hiring someone at that hourly wage while still keeping your share of the pie, the owner's profit.

If you can outsource the entire product creation process for $100 per unit, allocate $100 for marketing and operations, and $100 for your profit as an owner. Your goal then would be to sell your product for $300, adhering to the Rule of ⅓ (⅓ for production, ⅓ for marketing and operations, and ⅓ for profit). Skylar didn't need to allocate ⅓ for marketing and functions because of the strong social media presence. A significant marketing budget must be earmarked for a business without website traffic for customer acquisition (paid ads, affiliate marketing, search engine optimization, etc.). Without website traffic, customers will not find your product, and therefore, will not purchase it.

Gabi built the Rule of ⅓ into the process. The author earns a 35% royalty, and Amazon keeps 65% to list the book on their website, print it, and manage the orders. Gabi, Lamar, and Pax have start-up costs to create the initial product. However, once designed or built, they can be sold multiple times without additional costs per unit, unlike Skylar's model. Lamar and Pax kept ⅓ of the profit, so they have the luxury of spending up to ⅔ for operations and marketing. Most likely, though, they'd probably be able to spend less than ⅓ to run and market their business and keep ⅔ as profit.

If you don't adhere to the Rule of ⅓, you won't be able to grow your business, you won't be profitable, and you won't be able to sell your business. If you don't separate yourself from work, you'll create a job for yourself instead of building an automated, scalable, saleable online business. This concept is crucial, so you may want to review this section to ensure it's clear for you.

After establishing the initial target price, ensure that you deliver significant value to your customer by adhering to the 10X Principle.

10X Principle

It's not hard to make $1. Suppose you can create a handy PDF report, Kindle eBook, presentation template, financial spreadsheet, data compilation, online calculator, or mobile app, and charge $1 for it. In that case, you need to sell it a million times to make $1,000,000. It's simple enough. However, if people will pay $10, you only need to sell it 100,000 times. Better yet, if priced at $100, you only need to convince 10,000 people to buy it. You might wonder, if the math is this simple, why not just price your product at $1,000 or even $10,000 so that you need to sell fewer units to get to $1,000,000? That's possible, but there are some caveats.

Selling a product under $50 will not give you much room to market it. You will also attract more customers who will require higher maintenance (questions, complaints, refunds, etc.). Frequently a lower priced product is perceived as a lower value. As an example, we used to sell a product for $300. When we increased the price to $400, we sold even more. A month later, we again increased the price to $500 for the same product. Guess what? We sold even more! So, there are benefits to selling a product at a higher price, but you need to test it for your specific situation.

A higher-end product that sells for $1,000 or more will most likely require a phone call. You can automate that process too and hire salespeople to close the sale, but that adds a human element that can be unpredictable. Plus, you need to hire, train, coach, retain, and manage them. Regardless of how much you sell your product, you need to adhere to the 10X Principle, as outlined next.

The 10X Principle means that if you sell a product for $100, it must provide ten times value (10X) to the customer. You can measure the benefits of solving a problem for someone qualitatively and quantitatively. If you have a training program that helps salespeople generate $10,000 in sales for their company, don't hesitate to price your product at $1,000. Similarly, if you have a lender database where new customers can find the best mortgage where they can save at least $5,000, you can charge them $500 to access it.

For results that cannot be measured quantitatively, highlight the qualitative aspects by focusing on the emotional benefits. Magnify the benefits by vividly highlighting missed opportunities in the past, what they are missing now for not doing anything, and what they will continue to miss if they don't solve their problem. Focus on their pains and pleasures. What are the pains of being overweight? Health complications. Clothes that don't fit. Can't play with their kids. Poor self-esteem. What would life be like if they lose weight now? They will have more energy and higher confidence. They will be delighted when they receive flattering compliments.

If you can't articulate your product's value or don't yet feel that it should be sold at a specific price, increase the transformation it will deliver to your customers and find other ways to communicate your product's value.

For example, if you have an online program to help job seekers write a better resume, add some modules to help them find hidden job postings and learn how to negotiate a higher starting salary. With minimal effort, you can add additional value to your base product. If your product is a SaaS or a subscription to a digital library, maybe you can extend their access from three months to one year. Your job as an entrepreneur is to make your customers realize that they will get 10X more than they will pay for the product.

The Repeatability Factor

Now that you have defined the product and set the price, ensuring that it adheres to the Rule of ⅓ and the 10X Principle, perform one more check using the Repeatability Factor before you move on to identify your ideal customer.

The Repeatability Factor requires you to address a series of questions to help refine your product definition. By answering these questions, you can eliminate future bottlenecks and reduce threats that can derail your business. Consider these questions:

Can you repeat the product consistently? Meaning, can you source or produce it always at will within the same delivery time, cost, and quality? If there is a capacity or manufacturing limit, can you quickly scale it if needed? Are there multiple vendors available?

Can you repeatedly bring in the same number of customers every month? Even if there is a physical limit, is it high enough that you will not easily or quickly hit a plateau?

Can the process for creating the first product support the design of additional related products? For example, if you are selling a digital product, how easy will it be to create another digital product? If you are selling succulent plants, can the same model be used to sell office plants with minimal effort?

Lastly, can you repeatedly sell to the same customer? As morbid as it may sound, you can only sell a coffin once for an individual. You can't even consider a buy-one-get-one (BOGO) offer. However, if you sell identity theft protection software, they will have to subscribe to it every month. Whenever possible, find ways to incorporate a subscription element into your product. Subscriptions will give you recurring revenue so that you don't have to start your income at zero every month.

Now that you have a reasonably reliable product concept, it's time to define the ideal customer. Where are they in the customer journey? What are their pains and pleasures? Can they afford your product? Let's find out.

CHAPTER 3

DEFINE THE IDEAL CUSTOMER

Everything we do in life is a journey, from birth to death. If you break down our existence, you'll notice milestones along the way, such as learning to walk, riding a bike, graduating from school, landing the first job, getting married, having a child, buying a van, mourning a loss, and retiring from a career.

Each milestone is the end of one journey and the beginning of the next. As an entrepreneur, your job is to zero in on a specific portion of the life journey. From a business perspective, identify a particular moment to inject your product to help your customer. Much like a life journey, a customer journey consists of multiple milestones.

Just like in life, the distance between each milestone varies. Some are very short, hours, or days, while others are relatively long, months or years. The question is, where along that path can you insert your product to help a customer get to the next milestone? To answer that question, we need to delve deeper into the customer journey, position the product closer to what we call the "bleeding neck," clarify the Five Ps, and provide clues to the Affordability Enigma.

Customer Journey

Various marketing models structure the concept of the customer journey. Some have four steps, and others have seven milestones. However, the general idea is the same in all versions. The customer journey starts with gaining awareness of a problem and ends with purchasing a product. Consider the following four milestones: problem awareness, solution awareness, solution selection, and product purchase. Your business will need to usher target customers along the landmarks, from awareness through to purchase.

A potential customer will reach the problem awareness milestone either through push or pull. They may become aware of their problem because someone pushed the information to them, either through advertising (television, radio, newspaper, social media, etc.) or other means (referred by a friend, discussed at an event, mentioned by a professional, etc.). Alternatively, a potential customer may pull information because of a symptom or curiosity to understand a particular situation better.

After they have identified their problems, the potential customer will start seeking possible solutions. They will search online, scan blogs, watch videos, read books, join groups, download resources, and so on. When they find potential solutions, they will move to the next step of selecting the best solution for their problem. They will compare possible solutions, read product reviews, and pick a product. Once they have chosen your product, you need to make it easy for them to complete the purchase. Provide social proof, offer a guarantee, and address potential objections while keeping the entire process simple.

A highly-optimized process can usher a total stranger into a high-ticket customer within 24 hours. The definition of a high-ticket offer varies, but we've repeatedly seen sales anywhere from $2,000 to $50,000 or more, completed end-to-end from a stranger to a paying customer, cash in hand, in less than a week.

Although you can take your time to usher potential customers from problem awareness to product purchase, it is in your best interest to expedite the process. Set the pace for your potential customers and focus on their "bleeding neck" problem. A couple who has been having frequent disagreements has a problem. Those arguments can jeopardize their marriage, and they will probably seek a solution to rectify it. As serious as it may sound, it's not what would be considered a bleeding neck problem. However, if they experience verbal assault, emotional abuse, physical harm, or spousal infidelity, it's a bleeding neck problem.

Bleeding Neck Problems

If someone has a bleeding neck because of a car accident, the victim will seek help from the first person on the scene. From a customer journey perspective, the victim went through the problem awareness and solution awareness phases in a matter of minutes. When the first person offered to solve the victim's problem, the solution selection phase went quickly. It was a matter of life and death.

Seconds later, the victim became a "customer" and reached the "product purchase" phase almost instantly. If you position your product closer to the bleeding neck problem, customers experiencing similar issues have a very high intent of picking a solution.

Let's go back to the quarreling couple example. The couple may not even realize or accept the existence of a problem. The couple could stay in the problem awareness phase for months or years while having petty disagreements. As the occurrences become more frequent, they may move into the solution awareness phase to stay for more months or years. Unless something significant happens, they may never leave this phase.

However, when they reach a significant turning point, they will try to find a solution within days or weeks, perhaps start a marriage counseling program or initiate a marriage separation. Position your product immediately before or at the precipice of that turning point. That's the "bleeding neck" for that couple or relationship.

People can be overweight and still live a happy and fulfilling life. However, being diagnosed with a significant illness resulting from carrying the extra weight can be a turning point. An employee may put up with an unfulfilling career for years or decades to pay the bills but draw the line after being yelled at by a mean manager. An entrepreneur may continue to operate a business even though it is only breaking even because they don't want to accept defeat or don't know what to do. Still, when they are at the brink of bankruptcy or experience debilitating stress, they will likely seek professional help to turn things around.

In all of these situations, the potential customers need a product, a solution to their problems, and they need the answer soon. As such, you need a way to find them. Identify their demographics so that you can be where you are required to offer help. Join them on their Point A so that you can usher them to their Point B. That's where the Five Ps comes into play.

Five Ps

There are two key reasons someone will buy your product. People will part ways with their hard-earned money because they have a problem that's causing them pain or they are longing for something that will give them pleasure, or both. Solve a problem to satisfy a need. Their purchase will either allow them to avoid pain or achieve happiness.

Once you understand the concept of pains and pleasures related to your customers, you'll have a clear path of what product to create and how to reach the target customers.

The Five Ps includes problem, persona, psyche, pain, and pleasure, and they can help you start drafting a digital product to sell. Think of someone, an individual, or an organization; what problem will you solve for them? As you think of your offer, think of the biggest problem that you can solve. It's easy to see how solving a more significant problem can translate into a higher income.

Who is impacted by that problem? The problem must be so painful, or the pleasure so appealing, that getting them to Point B will have a real impact on their lives.

Paint a detailed picture of that individual or organization. Age? Gender? Location? Size? Industry? Likes? Dislikes? That's what we call the persona, or avatar, for your target customer.

With the problem and persona defined, start thinking about what might be going through that person's head. Are they thinking of personal gain? Do they feel that they're missing out on something? What logical thinking, realizations, and rationalizations are going through their heads?

What are their pains? What can they not do, perform, or achieve because they don't have your product?

What pleasures do they want to experience? Sense of stability? Belonging? Recognition? Physical strength? Mental clarity?

All of these factors are important in defining your product and marketing it.

The Affordability Enigma

There are two aspects to your product's price, a puzzle that you need to solve to help your customers overcome the fear of purchasing it. The first aspect is yours, and the second is the customers. The definition of "affordability" is different for everyone, and you need to understand your beliefs about it first. Take care of your side of the puzzle to help potential customers conclude that they can afford your product.

Once you have incorporated the Rule of ⅓, the 10X Principle, and the Five Ps into your product, then you are halfway to solving the Affordability Enigma. If you are still not convinced about your product and its price, go back and revisit your self-limiting beliefs and work on mastering your mindset. Once you have that in order, you can focus on the customer's perspective, broken down into quantitative and qualitative components.

As per the 10X Principle, you need to provide ten times the value to your customers. You can quantify the amount based on the benefits that they will gain and the cost of not solving the problem now. Highlight the cost-benefit analysis based on the past, present, and future. By not purchasing your product to solve their problem, how much have they missed in the past? What are they missing now? How much longer can they afford not to solve it?

If you know a unique salary negotiation technique that has helped job seekers gain an average uptick of 10% in income, how much money have they lost for not knowing it five or ten years ago? How much more will they miss this year? If they have 15-20 years left in their career, that's a significant amount. Even with an average income of $30,000, that would be an extra $3,000 in revenue this year alone. Quantitatively, then, it's a no brainer to charge $300 to share your secret with someone.

Moving to qualitative arguments, someone who's making 10% more will feel more valued, provide more for their families, and enjoy a better life. You can highlight the pleasure that they will gain as a result of your product. At the same time, you can demonstrate how your work will reduce their pain. In doing so, you will help your customers solve the Affordability

Enigma. They will convince themselves that they need your product. Even if they cannot afford it, they will find ways to buy it, especially if you make them acutely aware of their bleeding neck problem.

★ ★ ★ ★ ★

You have read this far. That's great!

If you think this book deserves a five-star review, can you please post your comments on Amazon to let others know?

If not, please contact me at https://johnestrella.com, and I'll do my best to address your feedback so that we can make this book better.

—John

CHAPTER 4

CREATE A PRODUCT TO SELL

After identifying what you are passionate about, determining how much you would like to earn, conceptualizing your product, and understanding your target customers, we're now ready to look at the Automated Online Business (AOB) Model.

Ideally, you want to build a business with specific characteristics. However, not meeting all of the criteria doesn't mean that your dream business is a bad idea. Assess what's out there, educate yourself on the pros and cons, and then design a business model that's specific to your desires, abilities, and circumstances.

Create a product that has a low barrier to entry. If possible, create something you can fund and build on your own in a couple of months. Digital products are best because you can make them once and then sell them multiple times. They also provide the opportunity for bulk sales and recurring revenue, such as subscriptions. With digital products, you can run your business anywhere in the world without needing to be available during specific fixed working hours.

Minimize or eliminate the business' dependency on you or another staff by automating almost all processes. That means building evergreen website traffic sources, simplifying the customer intake process, offering self-serve functionality, delivering the product, and collecting feedback. Own the entire infrastructure end-to-end as much as possible. Design the simplest, shortest, and fastest customer journey.

Now you're ready to familiarize yourself with the AOB Model, perform your market research, apply the PIE Method, prioritize the product's features, and start building the Minimum Viable Product (MVP).

AOB Model

The Automated Online Business (AOB) Model consists of four steps: Website Traffic → Landing Page → Checkout Page → Product Delivery. Try to keep everything simple and stick to these four steps.

Website traffic will bring awareness to your product. It can come from a variety of sources.

- Search results (Google, YouTube, Quora, etc.)
- Social media (Facebook, LinkedIn, Pinterest, etc.)
- Influencers (Instagram, Twitter, TikTok, etc.)
- Referrals (affiliates, reviews, books, etc.)
- Contents (blogs, articles, vlogs, etc.)
- Paid ads (pay-per-click, recommended articles, remarketing, etc.)
- Traditional media (television, radio, newspaper, etc.)

When potential customers arrive at your website, present a landing page with vital elements to entice them to commit by including the following five components: unique selling proposition (USP), hero banner or image, clear benefits, social proof, and call to action (CTA).

The USP includes the main headline, a supporting headline, a reinforcing statement, and a closing argument.

The hero banner provides the context of your USP using an image or video.

Feature a clear summary of benefits and provide supporting details.

Offer social proof such as customer testimonials and product reviews.

Lastly, have one conversion goal: click a button, fill out a form, or buy your product.

There are several critical elements for a successful checkout page. Some best practices include prioritizing for mobile checkout, providing multiple payment options, and asking for minimum information while keeping the entire process super simple. Display trust signals, use a progress indicator and remove distractions. Continue to refine and simplify. There is an entire industry devoted to the science of conversion rate optimization or CRO. So, test, learn, test, and test more!

Market Research

To help with your market research, here are some examples of digital products that fit the AOB Model. The possibilities are endless.

For example, online courses can teach how to take better pictures, prepare for a certification exam, start a new career, plan a wedding, learn a new language, etc.

Digital libraries allow customers to access images, pictures, sounds, video clips, databases, templates, documents, fonts, designs, contacts, checklists, etc.

Electronic intellectual assets can take the form of business valuation spreadsheets, exam preparation data banks, customizable legal documents, medical protocols, audit checklists, etc.

Software-as-a-service (SaaS) offerings to help create product roadmaps, share sales documents, track behavioral anomalies, schedule appointments, etc.

Mobile apps to store recipes, eat healthily, stay fit, track menstrual cycles, record podcasts, receive job alerts, take notes, automate processes, etc.

Although not digital products strictly, books can be sold as PDF and fully automated using print-on-demand technology via Amazon Kindle and Audible.

Entrepreneurs often make the mistake of focusing on market size. While that's important, you should focus on what piece of the market you can service, where along the customer journey you can find your prospective customers, how to enter the market quickly, and how long the sale process is.

Here's an example of how to understand and narrow your market. If you decided to narrow down your research using Facebook Audience Insights, knowing that there are 31.7 million small businesses is not very useful.

However, knowing that you can target 20-25 million small business owners on Facebook helps refine your focus. Suppose your product caters to women entrepreneurs. In that case, you can narrow it down to 10-15 million and even zoom in to focus on African-American women to reduce the target market to 8-9 million people. Let's say that you want to sell an online tutorial for taking care of naturally curly textured hair, specifically to 25 to 40 years old and single. You still have a sizable market of 500-600K people.

With this much focus, your messaging and images can directly resonate with them. If you can convince 1% of them (5,000 to 6,000) to subscribe to your online hair care tutorial for $20 per month, you'd be looking at $100,000 to $120,000 per month. That's a million-dollar fully automated online business! It looks promising, so you jump to Google to see what searches are popular by entering "natural afro hair," and you discover that people are looking for products, wigs, hairstyles, extensions, salons near me, and treatment.

Digging deeper, you check out Google Trends to see if the demand in the past few years is going up or down. The search volume is relatively steady, and it's prevalent in Maryland and Georgia. You noticed that "shampoo" was a breakout, meaning that the search term grew by more than 5000%! Ponytail showed at +250% and hair styling product at +160%.

YouTube presented additional results: care, braids, bleach, and twists. On Amazon, people are looking for wigs, t-shirts, clips, products, and extensions. You checked out one of the books to read both positive and negative reviews. The positive reviews gave valuable insights into what people would like to see on this topic. You also took note of the negative thoughts so that you can address them in your product.

Along the way, you have been compiling a list of topics and features that you'd like to consider for your product. In terms of the customer journey, the search term "treatment" caught your attention. Someone looking for treatment knows that they have a problem or a bleeding neck, and they want to solve it. They are likely closer to a purchase decision than people who are merely looking for products. From a conversion speed perspective, this is an ideal situation.

It is also very likely that they are the sole decision-maker, so there is no need to get a requisition or bureaucratic approval, typical for large organizations or government agencies. If you focus on teenagers, they will likely ask their parents to buy it for them. If you focus on older adults, you may not be able to target them on Facebook. Because you concentrate on single business owners 25-40 years old earlier in your market research, they can likely afford your product. With everything lining up, you decided to prioritize your product's features using the PIE Method.

PIE Method

Using a simple three-step formula, the PIE Method (potential, importance, and ease) allows you to calculate the PIE score to prioritize a product's features. You will likely find other products similar to what you had in mind. That's good. It means that there is a market for it.

Find the top two to three competitors and list their features. You'll end up with roughly 10-12 major features. Double check the list against what you found in your market research. If you find a feature that's not available from one of your competitors, mark it as a new feature. Aim for about 3-5 new features.

Create the following columns: MVP v1, MVP v2, Competitor 1, Competitor 2, Competitor 3, Potential, Importance, Ease, and PIE Score. Your Minimum Viable Product (MVP) v1 must deliver "must-have" features, and v2 should have "nice to have" features. Go through each component. Indicate a "Y" (yes) or "N" (no) for each element for your MVPs as well as your competitors.

For the potential, indicate how the feature's potential can improve your business's bottom line using a scale of 1 to 10, where one is low and ten is high. Do the same assessment on the importance of the feature to the business. Lastly, assess how you can easily incorporate the feature based on complexity, time, and cost. Add up the PIE numbers and divide by 3 to arrive at the PIE score. Start building your MVP based on the PIE score's descending order.

Minimum Viable Product (MVP)

Digital products can be simple, such as a checklist or a template, moderately complex, such as a digital library or online course, or very sophisticated, such as a mobile app or software-as-a-service (SaaS). You have three general options to create your MVP: build, license, or outsource.

For something simple, you can likely build it on your own. Suppose you have a downloadable PDF, a spreadsheet calculator, or a social media calendar. In that case, you can even host it on PayPal so that you can integrate the payment processor and electronic delivery in one spot.

You'll need a website to host the content and control access for a digital library or an online course. Depending on your degree of technical expertise, you can build it on your own or hire a developer to set it up for you. You can find developers on Fiverr, Guru, Upwork, and other freelance websites. There are also several choices for the platform, such as WordPress and LearnDash, or you can opt for a single integrated provider such as Teachable, Thinkific, Kajabi, or Ontraport.

When it comes to content, you can license a portion of it from the intellectual property owner. Search private label rights (PLR). You can reach out to private-label vendors. They offer electronic content such as articles, e-books, b-roll footage, and more, so you don't have to create your product from scratch. In some cases, you can just add a logo to make it your own.

If you need a physical product, there are private label manufacturers and wholesalers. Start with

Alibaba. You can sell a product from their catalog, and in most cases, they can drop ship it directly from their factory to your customers. Just like PLRs, if you want to add your logo to make it your own, that's possible too.

If you would instead not develop the MVP yourself, you can outsource the process to a freelancer or an agency and decide whether you want the provider to be local or offshore. If your digital product is simple, an individual contractor may be able to deliver the real MVP. In most cases, though, different specialties are required, such as writing, designing, filming, and packaging. Hiring an agency to coordinate the various specialists is an option. Along with that, you need to decide whether to hire someone local or offshore.

Each option has pros and cons, but hiring someone local makes it easy to communicate expectations and resolve issues—and more likely, they are in your time zone and working when you are. They are also more attuned to regional differences, sensitivities, and nuances. There are excellent offshore providers, as well. They may present communication and time zone issues, but you may save on cost with them.

For front-facing deliverables in English (writing, speaking, editing, etc.), you'll be better off with local providers. However, don't underestimate the capabilities of former British colonies in Africa. In contrast, there are excellent graphic designers and technical specialists, at much lower costs, in Eastern Europe and Asia, and they are typically fluent in English. Now that you have a plan for producing your product and before you get started, it's crucial to ensure you have your business correctly structured.

CHAPTER 5

FORMALIZE THE BUSINESS

Employees primarily get paid through salaries based on a predetermined amount by the employer. The employer is a business entity that is separate and distinct from the employee, a private entity. Most business owners mistake not separating these two different entities, business and personal, employer, and employee, respectively.

This foundational mistake can lay the groundwork for multiple issues down the road, with legal and financial ramifications. As such, it is imperative to formalize your business right at the beginning, separating your roles as the business owner and the first employee. Initially, you will likely perform both functions, owner and employee, but you must instill conceptual and physical separation when you start your business.

As an owner, you will invest financial and intellectual capital and other intangible assets such as connections, credibility, and inspiration. As an employee, you will likely wear multiple hats such as writer, editor, designer, developer, tester, marketer, bookkeeper, and more. However, for taking the risks of starting a venture, the owner is entitled to the profits. Based on the Rule of ⅓, as discussed previously, it is crucial to focus on profit first to ensure that it's embedded into the development, delivery, and profitability of the product to continue to grow at a sustainable pace.

As the business grows, you can replace one of your roles, the first employee, with someone else. In doing so, you have taken yourself out of the operational work so that you can focus on "owning" the business while continuing to collect the profits. When this moment arrives, you'll experience what actual business ownership is all about. Because your business can run without you (you have replaced your employee role with someone else), your business has value.

Because your business has value, someone may want to buy it, should you wish to sell it later on. There are various names and calculations to determine the selling price. Still, the profits you have carved out can be roughly considered the SDE (Seller's Discretionary Earnings) or the EBITDA (Earnings Before Interest Taxes, Depreciation, and Amortization). Those with MBAs will likely cringe at this analogy, but it is close enough for this discussion. And again, there are various complex calculations but depending on your business and its industry, and your buyer's needs and motivations, they may offer 3X to 4X the SDE or EBITDA. In the technology space, the buyer may even offer up to 10X. As the name implies, the third book on this trilogy, *Sell an Automated Online Business: Maximizing the Selling Price*, will guide you how to do it.

Let's say you have a business with gross sales of $1,000,000, and because you diligently adhered to the Rule of ⅓, your company has a profit of $333,333 or higher. At 3X to 4X multiples, you can expect to get an offer between $1M and $1.33M to purchase your business. There are plenty of caveats, but by professionally structuring your business, you will be in a better position to scale and sell it. To do this, pay close attention to how you fund your business, create a legal entity, open bank accounts, and establish merchant accounts.

Funding your business

You can start a business from zero by investing sweat equity into it. Let's say that you like food, so you decided to contact local restaurants in your area. You offer to write a review for them on Google, Facebook, and Yelp in exchange for free food. When you arrive, ask your server to take some pictures and videos of you with the chef and the owner. Enjoy the meal and post your reviews on Instagram, YouTube, and TikTok. Repeat this process 4-5 times. Use the pictures and videos with the chef and the owner as social proof and continue to approach more restaurants.

As your social proof grows, it will get easier to reach out to more restaurants. Eventually, they will start reaching out to you. To boost your influence even faster, invite other local influencers and news reporters to join you when visiting these restaurants.

To start monetizing it, you can invite 7-8 of your food connoisseur followers to join you for a special meal at a particular restaurant. Charge $45 for each meal, pay the restaurant $30 and keep the remaining $15 so you'll end up with $105-120 in profit. If you do it every day, you'll make between $3,150 and $3,600 per month, and you have a free meal in a restaurant every day! You can use your profit to fund your automated online business or just continue to refine it by automating most processes.

Let's take a look at another example. Assume that you need someone to take care of your mom while working at the office during the day. After searching for "adult daycare near me" on Google, you noticed no paid ads on the search results. Sensing an opportunity, you contacted all of the providers in your city and made arrangements to send a referral for $1 for each e-mail or phone inquiry. You also convinced them to pay you a $100 commission if someone signs up for a three-month contract.

So, you decided to run Google ads for $10 per day to generate 10-12 inquiries. When they see the ad, they can click a link to fill out a form or connect by phone. You created an online form that automatically forwards the inquiry to a provider via e-mail. Alternatively, if they click on the phone number, they will get connected directly to the provider. Even if no one becomes a customer, the referral fee will offset the daily ad spend so you can virtually run your ads forever. If you get one conversion for every 10-12 inquiries, you'll make $100 a day, automatically.

These are two simple examples of how you can bootstrap your business. The first one takes a bit longer to ramp up. The second example can be up and running within a day, and you'll see immediate results. If you'd like to generate more revenue faster, consider investing in a coach. A coach will cost between $1,000 and $15,000 (and up) and guide you through the process to avoid costly mistakes. Entrepreneurs often lose thousands of dollars due to avoidable errors that could have been prevented had they invested in a coach. New entrepreneurs also waste valuable time due to trial-and-error.

Be careful with coaching offers on the lower end because they tend to be incomplete. For example, the coach may show you how to run Facebook Ads or create a landing page. If hiring a coach, get help for the entire end-to-end process because a failure or weakness in one of the steps can translate into a disaster for your business. If you don't have enough money to invest, raise some cash through one of the previous examples. If you don't want to wait and you have access to credit, that's another option.

You'll need money to register your business, pay for some operating costs, and fund your marketing campaigns. As such, line up your financial resources first. Have about $10-15K in savings or credit. You may not need all of it to begin, depending on your business model. However, it's good to feel secure when you are starting a new venture. Otherwise, you'll run into a scarcity mindset that can impact your business's ability to focus.

Create a legal entity

There is a bit of a chicken-and-egg scenario in the spirit of separating business and personal entities right initially. You'll need a mailing address to register a company. You need a bank account to pay for the registration. But, you can't open a bank account without a legal entity and a mailing address, and they often also won't accept a post office box as your address.

Additionally, you'd want to pick a company name where the domain name and social media handles are still available for branding purposes. However, you can't be sure if you can register it as a business name if you found one.

To get around these challenges, settle on one preferred business name and one to two alternate names. Check the domain names and social media handles for availability. Ask your lawyer to perform a business name search. If everything turns out fine, then find a virtual mail service or virtual business address near you. Put it under your preferred business name, use your home address, and pay for it using your credit card.

Depending on your lawyer's advice, form your business as a sole proprietorship, partnership, limited liability company, or business corporation. There are pros and cons for each structure, so it is best to seek professional help to determine what is best for you. Depending on where you live, there are also different business structures along with corresponding tax implications. Register it using your virtual business address.

Once the business entity is in place, work with an accountant to determine what other local, regional, and national tax registrations are required. Then you can open company bank accounts.

Open bank accounts

It may take a few days before you receive your business and tax documents. The bank will ask for them, so have them available when you go there. Open a business checking account and a business credit card.

Your first deposit will be the seed funding so you can extend a "personal loan" to the company for, say, $5,000. Using the business checking account, reimburse yourself for what you paid for the virtual business address. Replace your credit card with the new business credit card so that future charges go into it. Pay your lawyer and accountant using the business checking account or business credit card.

From here on, only use the business credit card to pay for everything related to the business. Do not use it for personal use at all. If a vendor does not accept a credit card, send an electronic transfer, or write a check from the business checking account. When your business starts making money, it can pay back the seed funding that you initially loaned to it. At that point, the company is fully independent, and it doesn't owe any money to anybody.

In some cases, you will need to pay using Stripe or PayPal. That's fine as long as you connect them to the same business checking account and business credit card. We'll talk about Stripe and PayPal next.

Establish a merchant account

With the introduction of Stripe, you no longer need to integrate various systems to accept payments online. The flow used to be cardholder, merchant, merchant account/gateway, acquiring bank/processor, card networks, and issuing bank. It used to be a multi-step roundtrip process for each transaction and a cumbersome technical integration before you could accept your first payment.

Now, you can open a Stripe account online and be up and running right away. Stripe accepts the card holder's payment and deposits the amount into your business checking account a few days later. Stripe works with popular online shopping carts so you can accept online payments within days.

Make sure that you also open a PayPal account. Connect it to your business checking account and business credit card. If you are selling a downloadable product (e.g., PDF document) or you have some sort of an inventory (physical product or webinar attendance limit), PayPal can help manage it. Eventually, you'll need to pay contractors and other providers, sometimes in a different currency. You can use PayPal to pay them if they can't accept your electronic transfer, business check, or credit card payment.

Both Stripe and PayPal now allow the sending of electronic invoices to customers via e-mail. When they receive it, they can pay it directly online without you being part of the process. With both Stripe and PayPal connected to your business checking account, the payment will automatically show up a few days later.

With this setup, you will keep your bookkeeper and accountant happy. It will also be straightforward for you to monitor your business's financial health and focus on your product and customers rather than your business's administrative aspects.

CHAPTER **6**

BUILD YOUR SALES FUNNEL

A business exists to make money. You want to leverage your passion for building a business. Some entrepreneurs have altruistic reasons for starting a business, and that's good. But don't lose track of the fact that it has to generate profit. To do so, you need to serve your customers well, and we've already talked about how to do that—present a professional image. Help them trust your business. Make the process extremely easy when they are ready to buy. Most importantly, ensure that you deliver 10X the value for what they paid for your product and that you keep ⅓ as profit.

Your top priority should be to make your business profitable. With enough cash, your company can solve more problems—higher compensation for your staff, a better working environment, and more options to pursue your altruistic goals or social causes. Most entrepreneurs focus on these items in the wrong order. They focus on getting more social media followers, winning industry awards, participating in community development, and so on at the expense of generating profit first.

For a business to have a continuous and predictable profit flow, it needs to have a sales funnel. A well-oiled sales machine must present a professional and consistent brand while capturing data for business analytics. Your marketing assets must align with the brand. Usher the customer from awareness to purchase by presenting an integrated end-to-end journey using the logo, color, image, tone, and typography. Building that flow will require testing and continuous optimization after the initial launch. With the end-to-end flow in place, your business is ready to receive customers, make sales, generate profit, and use that profit to grow the company more.

Define the brand guidelines

Large corporations spend thousands of dollars, sometimes even millions of dollars, building and promoting their brands. That's understandable, given that valuable brands are worth billions of dollars—

think Amazon, Google, and Apple. Others are considered high-value brands, such as Louis Vuitton, Hermes, and Gucci. For your small business, keep it simple and start with the logo, color, image, tone, and typography.

You'll need to choose four colors: primary and secondary colors, along with complementary dark and light colors. Use the primary color, and optionally the secondary color, on the logo. Stick to these four colors when designing your marketing assets (website, graphics, ads, etc.).

Keep in mind that colors have corresponding symbolism: red for love, passion, or lust; blue for serenity, stability, or wisdom; green for nature, healing, or fertility; and so on. Use the color of the sun, yellow, if you want to convey sunshine or joy. Also, be aware that colors have different symbolic meanings in other cultures, and be sure to cross-check based on your target audience.

What image would you like your business to project? Formal or friendly? Affordable or expensive? Mysterious or approachable? How you want to launch your business will influence the tone of your messages, such as website content, e-mail communications, marketing taglines, and more. Lastly, adhere to particular typography to make your text legible, readable, and appealing. Carefully select the font types, point sizes, and line spacing.

From these brand guidelines, graphics designers can create fantastic marketing assets to build the sales funnel.

Prepare the marketing assets

A simple sales funnel comprises a traffic source, landing page, payment page, and confirmation page. Create your marketing assets (text and visual) by tightly aligning these four elements. Suppose the traffic source (search engine results, paid ads, social media posts, etc.) says "Tobermory wreck diving." In that case, the landing page must immediately confirm that they are viewing a page about scuba diving for shipwrecks in Tobermory. From there, customers can purchase a related product by entering payment information. Upon credit card payment approval, display the confirmation page, deliver the product (download or access an electronic product, or ship it if it's a physical product).

Depending on the traffic source, you may need to prepare different marketing assets. To keep things simple, stick to the core elements: text (message or caption), visual (image or video, if applicable), and call to action (CTA). For example, a Google text ad will need a headline, display URL, and description. These are all text elements.

In contrast, a Facebook ad or a social media post needs text, visual, and CTA. The graphic will catch the viewer's attention. It will help if you compel the reader to skim the text to take action. The text and visual must complement each other. So, if the text says "Wreck Diving $499", the graphic should have a picture of a scuba diver exploring a wreck. The CTA may say, "Book My Dive." Although a visual with a photo or video of a beach may evoke a feeling of relaxation, it is not as tightly complementary to the text compared to a graphic of a scuba diver with a wreck in the background.

Because the text element may have multiple length limitations (headline, description, CTA, etc.), your marketing assets (or marketing war chest) must have an inventory of text in various lengths for each type. A headline may say "Diving $499", "Wreck Diving $499", "Tobermory Wreck Diving $499", and so on. The description may state "includes all equipment rentals, boat, and divemaster to explore the Niagara II and Arabia shipwrecks" or a shorter "two deep dives; equipment and boat included."

The graphic designer must trim the visual to various sizes for different purposes, e.g., rectangle vs. square. For example, for Facebook ads alone, be prepared to display the images in several places such as mobile vs. desktop news feed, the marketplace, stories, right column, and search results. Ensure that you have an adequate inventory of these marketing assets.

After preparing your marketing assets for the traffic source, start building the landing page. You'll need a combination of text, visual, and CTA to make the landing page appealing and compelling. Come up with a unique selling proposition (USP), select a hero image or video, and a list of your offer benefits. You'll also need some form of social proof such as testimonials, social media followers, and so on. There must be a single, clear conversion goal.

For the checkout page, keep it simple. Remove distractions and only ask for what's required to complete the purchase: e-mail, credit card number, expiration date, and credit verification code (CVC), sometimes called card verification value (CVV). After a successful payment, direct the customer to the confirmation page with instructions on how they can access the product or what will happen next.

Integrate the end-to-end flow

The sequential flow from the traffic source, landing page, payment page, and confirmation page is reasonably straightforward. Visitor clicks on a link (search results or paid ads), arrives on the landing page, decides to buy the offer, pays for it, and receives what was purchased. The payment page will need to be connected to accept payment, typically PayPal, Stripe, or some other providers. Set it up to automatically deposit into the company's checking account when a payment is received.

The confirmation page may trigger a series of events such as displaying a download link, providing online access, or starting an e-mail sequence. Identify what must be completed based on your business and set it up correctly. For example, going back to our wreck diving example, the confirmation page may say to look for an e-mail with all the details. As such, a payment confirmation e-mail may be sent automatically by the credit card processor. However, you'll need to set up an e-mail sequence with links to more information about the dive sites and various electronic forms. You may also want to collect additional information such as diving certification details, medical history, and so on.

Test the customer journey

With the customer journey designed, traverse the "happy path" (positive tests) by performing an end-to-end test. Go through from the beginning to the end like a typical customer, not encountering any issues at all. View the traffic source and check all elements (text, visual, and CTA). Click on the CTA to go to the landing page. Check all of the pieces again and then click on the CTA to purchase the product. Enter the credit card details. After approval, deliver the product. Did the e-mails get sent?

Test as many negative scenarios as you can imagine, such as missing fields, invalid credit cards, out of inventory, and so on. Your merchant processor can typically provide test credit card numbers to help you with testing. Additionally, there might be an option to set the flow to "test mode" so that you can go from start to finish without an actual credit card charge. Once everything is in order, you are ready to open your business. Congratulations!

CHAPTER **7**

OPTIMIZE THE CUSTOMER EXPERIENCE

Creating a product and getting your customers to buy it is half the battle. The other half requires you to continue the fantastic customer journey after they parted with their hard-earned money. Simply put, they placed their trust in you. You now need to deliver value.

Becoming a millionaire or a billionaire is not as simple as achieving a financial milestone. It's about not letting your customers down because they trusted you. They have a big problem to solve, be it personal or professional, and they expect your product to solve that problem. And we're not talking about one or two individuals. It's hundreds or thousands of people, hopefully even more.

Taking care of your customer is a big responsibility. Just as you made it easy for them to purchase your product, make it easy for them to benefit from it. To do this, you need to create an onboarding process, allow them to help themselves, establish a ticketing system, and measure whether they are happy with your product or not.

Craft an onboarding process

An onboarding process does not need to be complicated. Essentially, you want to welcome your new customers. Thank them for their business and set the expectations on what they can expect in the coming days or weeks. It can be a simple e-mail that tells them how to start using your product.

What's their username and password? If they can't find it, give clear instructions on how to find it. If needed, show them how to reset their passwords. You might also offer them links to helpful instructional videos, point them to a frequently asked questions (FAQ) page so that they can help themselves. If they cannot solve the problem themselves, encourage them to contact the help desk and tell them when they can expect a response. Provide various ways for them to reach your business: e-mail, phone, chat, etc.

If you have a subscription product that renews every month, ensure that they see the benefits right away to encourage them to keep renewing their subscriptions. If you offer drip access, tell them when and how new content will be available to them. For example, you can say that they will not have access to the second module until after completing the first module.

After onboarding, continue to deliver value to your customers by allowing them to help themselves. Make it easy for them to find answers to their questions on their own. It will be challenging to have an automated online business if they need to rely on you for everything.

Let them help themselves

When customers run into a problem with your product, they want answers right away. Most of the time, however, your customers will ask the same questions over and over again. So, start with a handful of issues your customers may encounter and craft a response or solution for each one of them. Compile them on a FAQ page and make sure to provide a link to it as part of your onboarding process.

You can also offer a chatbot to provide canned responses to common inquiries such as your address, phone number, support e-mail, what products you offer, and how to find the FAQ. With an FAQ and a chatbot, you'll be able to respond to most of the issues while providing superior customer service quickly.

You can also create an online community where customers can interact with each other. Carefully plan and monitor the interactions because it will only take one disgruntled customer to inject negativity into the platform. Encourage them to post celebrations and successes. Doing so will foster positivity instead of negativity. If you see a negative post, consider deleting it right away and privately reaching out to that customer.

If their question is still unanswered, then they can submit a ticket. So, let's talk about that next.

Provide a ticketing system

There are various names for a ticketing system. Others might call it a help desk software, a service management platform, a support center, and so on.

First, customers can search the FAQ or connect using a chatbot. If that doesn't resolve the issue, they need a way to get support. A ticketing system will catalog and track the issue and assign it to someone who can fix it.

Some features to look for in a ticketing system are omnichannel support, ticket assignments, workflow automation, reporting and analysis, and knowledge base. By having omnichannel support, you can use the same ticketing system to manage e-mail, phone, chat, in-person, social media, and other ticket sources all in one place. Ticket assignments enable distribution to team members best equipped to solve the problem. It also usually supports ticket categorization and prioritization. With workflow automation, streamline certain processes using macros to complete specific tasks with minimal human intervention. You also need to generate reports to analyze common problems and find ways to eliminate or minimize them. Lastly, there should be a way to store, search, and share the knowledge base.

Although profitability can serve as a positive indicator of customer satisfaction, along with a well-managed ticketing system, they only present one side of the equation. To honestly know if your customers are satisfied, you need to ask them by measuring the net promoter score (NPS).

Measure the net promoter score (NPS)

On a scale of 0 to 10, the net promoter score (NPS) measures the percentage of your customers who are satisfied with your product and who will likely recommend it to friends. Those who rated your product as 9 or 10 are called promoters. In contrast, customers who provided a rating of 6 or lower are considered detractors. NPS ignores ratings of 7 or 8 (passives). Subtract the percentage of promoters from the detractors to calculate the NPS.

The NPS range can be as low as -100 (all are detractors) or as high as 100 (all are promoters). Scores vary across industries, but anything higher than zero is considered acceptable, 50+ as excellent, and 70+ exceptional.

As part of your onboarding process and ticketing system, inject NPS checkpoints along the way. You may want to measure their satisfaction shortly after buying the product, when you close a ticket or after they finished using your product. This process will allow you to measure the change of sentiment along the customer journey.

It is crucial to reach out to detractors to understand their dissatisfaction. Get to the root cause of the problem and proactively address them immediately to prevent permanent brand damage or erosion. Passives are susceptible to switching to competitors, so like the detractors, find ways to convert them into promoters.

Take care of your promoters just as much as you take care of your detractors and passives. Find out what they like the most about your product and make those things even better for future customers. Promoters can also help you build your social proof, so ask them to rate your company and product on various review websites. Video testimonials add more credibility.

It will be easier to convert customers into your company's cheerleaders if your company has excellent NPS.

★ ★ ★ ★ ★

If you still have questions that I haven't addressed so far, please don't hesitate to contact me at https://johnestrella.com.

If you haven't done so already, I'd greatly appreciate it if you can give this book a glowing review on Amazon. Thank you so much for your support!

CHAPTER 8

CONVERT CUSTOMERS TO CHEERLEADERS

You'll find getting the first customer reasonably tricky for someone who's starting a business from scratch. If you look back through your journey, you spent time trying to identify your passion. You figured out how to leverage your power to solve a problem for someone. With the problem defined, you identified your ideal customer, which set the foundation for your product.

After creating your product, you formalized your business and built a sales funnel to ensure a steady customer stream. As you bring in customers, you put processes in place to ensure that they have the most fantastic experience with your company and your product. From an academic standpoint, it sounds great.

But how do you get your first customer? And then grow your business from there?

As a new business, you have no credibility. You have no success stories. Most business owners are aware of this significant startup issue. That's why they spend so much time building their facade, as shallow as it may seem, by beefing up their social media profiles. They spend time and money to host webinars, shoot videos, record podcasts, post blogs, and so on.

Therein lies the problem. These entrepreneurs are building their social proof first, instead of last, as we are doing here. We made the product first so that when we unleash the webinars, videos, podcasts, and blogs, we have a systematic and cohesive messaging approach to sell our product. We will build our social proof with a purpose and not just to collect followers, likes, and shares from people who may not even buy our product.

To start, use your existing social media presence and reach out to your friends and family to become pilot customers. Usher them through the entire customer journey. Show them what a potential customer may see from the traffic source (e.g., paid ads) to the landing page. Provide them a unique discount code so that they don't have to pay the full price. You need to make sure that they have to pay, even if it is just for a minimal amount. Otherwise, they will not have skin in the game.

Imagine being able to convince five of them to be your pilot customers. It shouldn't be that hard. In turn, they will tell five friends. Three of those five friends might decide to sign up, who, in turn, tell five of their friends. As you can see, you can quickly grow your business through word of mouth, which is the easiest, cheapest, and fastest way to scale your business. But you need to have a deliberate process to make it happen. And it starts by getting feedback from your customers.

Get feedback from customers

Set the stage for a closed feedback loop, starting with your onboarding process. It can be as simple as asking your customers how they found you (traffic source), what their motivation is for buying your product (intent), and what compelled them most to pick your product over your competitors (sales copy).

Expect skewed data with your pilot customers, but because you are building this process as part of your entire customer journey, you'll get more meaningful results over time. Use the data to identify profitable traffic sources, adjust your messaging to align with their intent, and highlight key product differentiators significant to customers.

As they use your product, ask them what they like most and what can be improved. Capture the data into a product backlog to prioritize for upcoming releases of your work. Whenever a customer submits a support ticket, look for ways to prevent receiving a similar ticket in the future, perhaps add the information in your onboarding process or include it in the FAQ.

After you close a ticket, use the opportunity to measure the NPS. If they rate your business 9 or 10, they are your promoters. Invite them to write an online review and make sure to ask for a video testimonial too. The more comfortable you can make this process, the more likely it is that they will do it for you, e.g., please record a short video on your phone and e-mail it to us.

Passives gave a score of 7 or 8. Find out what you can do to convert them into promoters. For example, with an online exam preparation product, a customer joined who had previously bought a competitor's product and failed the exam. The customer was upset and was taking out their frustrations on the new product. The customer submitted 24 tickets in two hours. The team politely and promptly responded to each one. When the last ticket came, they included the usual macro, asking for feedback. The customer was so happy. They gladly posted a long positive review of our product and superior customer service.

For a feedback score of 6 or lower (detractors), pick up the phone, and be a regular human being. Recognize their concerns. Don't judge. It doesn't matter if you agree or disagree with their problems. If they feel that way, that's their reality. It's real for them. The best thing that you can do is to listen and possibly learn. Sometimes, they just need to vent their frustrations. In the end, ask the question, "What can I do to make this right for you?" Agree on a resolution, and do it.

On several occasions, it makes the most sense to issue a full refund. Sometimes, it's cheaper to do that than to keep a disgruntled customer who can give you so much aggravation and bad PR. Do not take it personally. Instead, shift your attention to serving your dream customers—and if you learned something, use it to improve.

Encourage promoters to tell their friends about your product. It's similar to what you did when getting started with your friends and family.

Encourage them to tell their friends

An affiliate program can serve as a core traffic source in an automated online business. Although it is a long-term game, it is an inexpensive and effective way to generate revenue because you don't have to pay them until after. Affiliate marketing is a different topic beyond the scope of this book. However, it can be used at a basic level to ask existing customers to tell their friends about your product.

You can ask existing customers to sign up as affiliates. In doing so, they'll get a unique link that they can share with friends. The affiliate marketing software keeps track of conversions, and you can pay them a commission for referring friends to become customers.

As well as asking a happy customer for a video testimonial, you can also schedule a video interview with that happy customer to gain insight into their motivation, address common objections from potential customers, and compare "before" and "after" results of using your product. You can add these interview videos to your marketing assets. Customers can also share them with friends and family with an affiliate link, so they also receive a referral commission. If they have a strong social media presence, encourage them to share it through those channels.

Create a supportive community

Along the line of creating the best customer journey to encourage satisfied customers to tell their friends and family, building a supportive community is also essential. Others call it a tribe, a group of tight-knit, like-minded people who are passionate about your business or product. Create a place where your customers can interact, such as a Facebook or LinkedIn Group. Visit https://johnestrella.com to join our group.

Establish community guidelines to maintain a positive vibe within the group, set the stage to keep the community positive and helpful, and encourage members to ask and answer questions. Use this opportunity to demonstrate your expertise or show how your product will solve their problem. If a community member provides an incorrect response, correct it nicely while helping them maintain their self-esteem and shift the discussion to your product. It is a tough balancing act between helping and selling, so be cautious with your posts and when you reply.

Prohibit promotional materials, affiliate links, or self-promotion spams in posts or comments. Indicate that several admins monitor the group to ensure that members get the most value. Ensure that admins also quickly remove posts that violate the community guidelines. Remind the community members to be kind always.

Use this online community to nurture prospective customers and establish your credibility. It is also an excellent channel to celebrate customer success. This community is also an appropriate place to share testimonial and interview videos. And with that, it's time to cover the last topic of this book: celebrating customer successes.

Celebrate customer successes

Your prospective customers may not tell you this, but at the back of their minds, they think that just because your product worked for someone else, it may or may not also work for them. Similarly, your product transformed your customers from their "before" into a new "after" situation. They may have been unemployed, and your online job search course helped them land their dream jobs. Maybe your online service can connect wealthy individuals to general contractors and enabled them to realize their dream homes finally. Celebrate these successes!

We all like human stories. They are authentic and credible. So encourage your customers to share their stories in the online community you have built.

They can share the same information with their friends also. You can even arrange to feature them in local and national news outlets.

Influencers are always looking for new content. Find influencers with followers who might be interested in your product but who themselves are not your competitors. Sign up these influencers as affiliates, and they can share your customer stories with their audiences, which is a win-win situation for both of you. You are helping the influencers create content and generate affiliate revenue, and they are helping you attract new customers while enhancing your credibility.

You Can Do This

Creating your own automated online business is both possible and achievable. That said, it's easier to describe and read how to build and launch an automated online business than to actually do it. There's no doubt about that. However, if you follow the steps in this book and genuinely commit to the process, you can turn your passion into your livelihood—and make the income you want.

Parts of this process are iterative, and you may need to go back a step as you work through this to adjust or course-correct along the way. But the time you invest is worth it—your efforts can result in the freedom and joy of doing what you love and making a good living. All you have to do is commit to the process and follow the steps. Go for it!

Index

Automated Online Business Books

Start an Automated Online Business: Turning Your Passions Into Millions

Paperback: 978-1-990135-00-2
Kindle: 978-1-990135-01-9
Audible: 978-1-990135-02-6

Scale an Automated Online Business: Unlocking and Perfecting Profitability

Paperback: 978-1-990135-03-3
Kindle: 978-1-990135-04-0
Audible: 978-1-990135-05-7

Sell an Automated Online Business: Maximizing the Selling Price

Paperback: 978-1-990135-06-4
Kindle: 978-1-990135-07-1
Audible: 978-1-990135-08-8

Solopreneur Programs

Apply to our programs by visiting our website.
https://agilitek.com/solopreneur

www.ingramcontent.com/pod-product-compliance
Lightning Source LLC
Chambersburg PA
CBHW071505200326
41519CB00019B/5872